MYSTERIES OF THE SOUL

By Louis Sefer

Copyright © 2023

Table of Contents

Introduction 5

The Search for the Soul 7

   Definition of the Soul 16

Religious and Ancient Beliefs of the Soul 20

   Religious Beliefs 20

   Ancient Beliefs 23

   Scientific Views 26

   Parapsychology 31

Metaphysical Viewpoints of the Soul 34

Origin of the Soul 43

The Soul's Purpose: Evolution 45

Age of the Soul 48

   The Caste System 49

The Planetary Initiatory System 53

The Chronological Aging System 58

Types of Souls 63

   The Moon or Lunar Type 65

   The Sun or Solar Type 66

   The Mercurian Type 66

The Venusian Type.....................................66

The Martian Type.....................................66

The Jupiterian Type...................................67

The Saturnian Type...................................67

The Neptunian Type..................................67

The Uranian Type 67

7-Ray Types 68

Soul and Immortality 71

Soul Faculties and Soul-Culture 75

Soul Faculties.......................................78

Soul Culture 79

Meditation 80

Energy-Work 81

Soul-Refinement 82

Conclusion 83

Introduction

We are currently living in a very complex era known to humanity's intelligentsia as the "Space Age," "Computer Age," "Atomic Age," "Information Age," and "Technological Age."

These are the concluding "Ages" of the Piscean period, which will soon give way to new developments. We will eventually hear terms or phrases like "Ascension Age," "Quantum Age," "Hyper-Space Age," and "Photon Age."

All of these subsequent Ages reference to and refer to the distinctive nature of the forces that will shortly interact, interface, and integrate with humanity in the future Aquarian Age, producing a transmutation inside man's psychosomatic system at the cellular and atomic levels.

Our genes' two-helix DNA structure will split and multiply into twelve strands according to the same logic that splits a cell. Certain atoms within the pineal gland, as well as certain parts of the brain, will become active at the same time.

The synapses and dendrites of the brain's neurons will develop new connections throughout the grey matter, connecting both the right and left hemispheres, as well as the cerebellum and the cerebrum. Chakras other than the primary seven would be aroused and anchored into man's lower force-field as well.

Furthermore, the different levels of the chakric-system and their myriad petals or qualities will bloom, bestowing man with unfathomable abilities. It is stated that attaining enlightenment is a chemical and electrical event as well as a psychological one. It is, in reality, an alchemical process.

In short, in the Aquarian Age, man will be spiritually transformed and made again to a higher level of perfection—but only if man is ready and works to help this. This transformation is the evolutionary quantum leap that humanity will experience.

With all of the amazing philosophical discoveries that will take place, there will still be simple realities that would need to be addressed to enlighten the layperson, such as the existence of the soul, which is the subject of this book.

There are many seekers and potential seekers of a higher reality who need to be led in the right direction. It is my sincere desire that this book may fill the void in people's minds about the hidden aspect of their existence, causing them to delve further into the amazing mysteries of the cosmos.

The Search for the Soul

The scientific search for the soul began with the rise of spiritualism in the early decades of the nineteenth century, when the Fox sisters claimed to have communicated with the spirit realm.

Despite all of man's "miraculous" high-tech advancements in these latter days of the Piscean Age, orthodox science has yet to adequately answer the question of the existence of the soul and its survival of bodily death.

The existence of the soul has not been academically and scientifically "confirmed" in the laboratory to the satisfaction of scholars from all fields of study; on the other hand, the non-existence of the soul has not been shown.

To our knowledge, instruments that monitor, measure, and scan frequencies outside the known energy-spectrum have yet to be invented before Science can provide clear confirmation of the existence of the soul.

Tesla and Edison's numerous inventions demonstrated that they were pioneers working on this subject.

Philosophers have speculated for ages on the existence of the soul and its survival of the body; its nature and relationship to the physical form; its origin and destiny; and its possibly exalted nature, or condition of immortality.

Intellectual and analytical thinking, on the other hand, have failed to give any substantial proof of an autonomous being existing apart from the physical body. Our global philosophers and intellectuals' genuine search for the soul through a priori, or reason alone, appears to have declined in the twentieth century.

Perhaps it is realized that the intellect has limitations in grasping, comprehending, and truly knowing abstract and metaphysical matters, or it could be realized that any concept that could be thought of has already been conceptualized—that any novel ideas would merely be variations of previous metaphysical speculations and theories, and would not make man any wiser.

This would reaffirm the everlasting fact that there is nothing new under the sun. Even so, there will always be zealots.

When it comes to determining the nature of Reality or the Absolute, the physical senses, mortal mind, and intellect are inadequate.

What is relative may be known intellectually and experienced objectively; relative absolutism may be speculated upon though without knowing whether one's conclusions are of the absolute truth in the absence of scientific proof, even if they be rational and logical; examples of this is the "Unified theory" of Einstein and the "Idealism" of Kant.

Absolute absolutism is inexplicable and ineffable. It transcends the intellect, and any normal description of it is merely deceptive.

Even the phrase "indescribable and ineffable" may be too strong. From the perspective of the Absolute, all we know, whether via our senses or intellect, is perhaps erroneous and illusory.

The Absolute is known as "Ain Sof" in the Qabala, the Hebrew/Jewish esoteric oral tradition. It is the unknown God, the Source of all that is not described in the exoteric scriptures. With his human traits, Jehovah, the god of Moses, is only a reflection of the supreme god found in the pantheons of the coexisting cultures of the period.

The existence and nature of Ain Sof were not made public because the Initiates realized that the masses' mental ability and spiritual growth had not reached the necessary degree for such revelations to be intuitively grasped and safely used. This situation still exists today, but with a twist.

Man's intellectual progress has now far exceeded his spiritual development. When discussing abstract topics, the human mind tends to concretize and anthropomorphize that which cannot be objectified or grasped intellectually; thus, man's failure to comprehend abstract matters leads him to conclude that they do not exist. As a result, man becomes unaware of his own ignorance.

Though the following notions about Reality appear to be distinct, they are in fact interconnected and linked with one's way of perception and intuitive insight.

On the surface, they are our various ideas or perceptions of Absolute Reality. We shall not conjecture further since the deeper we probe intellectually, the further we stray from the reality. Only by mystical means can reality be known and experienced.

What is the relationship between the soul and the notions mentioned above? Is the soul just another mental construct, or can it be understood and experienced in a physical and concrete way, or in any way that transcends the physical senses and intellect?

As the Piscean Age relies heavily on analytical reasoning to grasp "truth," the Aquarian Age will rely heavily on altered states of consciousness, intuition, and other higher faculties to perceive, experience, and comprehend abstract realities.

The factual knowledge gathered by each individual in an absolute state of awareness will determine whether intuition or a higher faculty establishes the presence of the soul.

We have no doubt that science will eventually confirm the existence of the soul, or certain aspects of it, at some point in the future, but the answer to such a question may be obtained here and now through mystical means.

The emphasis in the next Age will move from speculative metaphysics to applied metaphysics or practical mysticism.

Though this has already occurred with the various actions of proponents and exponents of occultism and metaphysics in recent decades, this state will worsen in the coming millennium. True knowledge of the soul must come from the soul itself. It can't be any other way. Science can only uncover a portion of it.

When Prometheus took fire from the gods and gave it to humanity, he guided humanity down the path of civilization and spiritual inquiry.

Many of primitive man's anxieties were alleviated by fire. With the discovery of fire, man could relax in the warmth of his cave for the first time in his life, without fear of being attacked by unforeseen predators.

Man began to contemplate and reflect on his newfound freedom. His higher mind began to awaken, and he began to question the existence of invisible worlds and a "self" apart from the material form. Certain experiences he experienced, such as dreams, psychological feelings, and incomprehensible instinctual knowledge, inspired this cogitation.

In his dreams, he felt that something within him emerges from the body to carry on with the activities of the day. This was the beginning of faith in the existence of the soul. Thus, the belief in and quest for an incorporeal principle of human life predates recorded history and can be found in all cultures in some form or another.

Only the spiritual cream of society—mystics and saints—have so far solved the riddle of the soul's existence via experimentation in the laboratory of the Spirit.

Mystics, sages, and prophets have stressed the necessity of understanding the immaterial entity that animates and guides the body throughout history. This entity is referred to by some as the mind, the self, the soul, the life-force, the spirit, the ego, the personality, the psyche, the Spark of God, and so on. They claim that recognizing this ethereal reality of man is the only way to realize one's Source and purpose for being.

The inherent impulse that inspires and impels man to seek the soul is derived from the enigmatic soul-factor itself. The importance of the quest is perceived by the mind, but the precise cause is unknown. Jung referred to this as the religious instinct. Furthermore, this "instinct" is seen not only in humans, but also in other primates and cetaceans.

Another intriguing truth is that higher animals exhibit many so-called human characteristics including remorse, shame, and pride. If these sentiments are related with the soul, then the soul, or at least the essence of the soul, may be considered to reside in animals as well. However, man is thought to be the only being who thinks about the soul, death, the afterlife, and so on. The American philosopher William Ernest Hocking (1873-1966) writes in his book *The Meaning of Immortality in Human Experience* that,

"Man is the only animal that contemplates death, and also the only animal that shows any sign of doubt of its finality."

Is there such a thing as a soul? And what is the significance of soul identification? Without the search for the discovery of the "soul," as well as awareness of its purpose of being, there would always be a sense of dissatisfaction and disquiet in man's bosom.

Without irrefutable confirmation of individual identity survival, life appears to be a succession of meaningless events and experiences. If the soul does not exist and everything ends with the death of the human form, then all of life's efforts and strivings are futile.

Why bother with life's hard teachings if everyone will be annihilated, with not a single iota of the immaterial man surviving the physical form? Suicide would be a convenient getaway; but, we have the impression that suicide violates cosmic rules—rules established by whom or what?

On the other hand, man's inflated ego has led him to assume that he is the only creature on the planet with a soul. His "high intelligence" demonstrates this.

Man believes that no other species has the same faculties as him, such as imagination, reason, and will—the essential qualities required to control and manage the environment. This reasoning gave man a sense of superiority and uniqueness, as well as a sense of being God's chosen one, for was he not created "in the image of God"?

This is essentially an egotistical viewpoint, one that leads to the exploitation, abuse, manipulation, and eventual annihilation of Nature.

This notion is linked to the assumption that intelligent life exists solely on Earth and that Man is a representative of it.

The ego has blinded man to the fact that life adapts to whatever circumstances it finds itself in. The chemical and environmental prerequisites for sentient life on Earth may not be the same as the requirements for life to appear on another planet. Other or undiscovered elements may support life.

For example, carbon, which is the basis of life on Earth, may not be the basis of life on other worlds. Other planets may alternatively use silicon, silica, or other minerals. It is not any of the recognized gases that give life, but the universal life-force known as prana.

Aside from that, from a metaphysical standpoint, life exists not only in the spectrum of energy that we objectively experience, but also beyond that. As an example, a planet like Venus or Pluto could be home to sentient people living in the planet's upper dimensions without being observed by rudimentary telescopes or tools we label technologically advanced, like the Hubble Space Telescope.

If man evolved self-identity out of the functions of the life-force, when did he acquire it? If the soul is considered an entity, when does it ensoul the form, or does it enter when the baby takes its first breath?

Such concerns can only be answered if we have a thorough understanding of the metaphysical aspect of life. The study and comprehension of all of nature's seemingly intangible aspects, such as the microcosmic constituents and functions of man—the etheric elements supporting organic life, the divine spiritual force that sustains the microcosmic structure, the three-fold Soul, and so on—helps greatly in answering profound questions.

Man has subconscious knowledge of his soul, but for some reason he actively blocks this out by "pretending" to be ignorant. He hypnotizes himself into rejecting immaterial reality since it is the path of least resistance for him. Actually, remembering is much easier than forgetting. The fact that we are looking for it proves that the soul, or spiritual essence of man, exists! It is the enigma of the soul's search for itself.

We recognize that this is a contentious matter, and because it is tied to religion, it has a certain level of sensitivity among religious extremists. This emotional sensitivity, however, should be set aside in the rationalistic study of the soul; for in order to acquire helpful information, one must be objective, open-minded, intelligent, tolerant, and careful.

Unrestrained emotionalism is a roadblock to discovering the truth. Hopefully, this paper will provide the reader with a better understanding of the mystery of the soul and our intense search for it.

This is a complicated subject, and it would be impossible to completely satisfy the intellect. Its sole objective is to stimulate the mystical consciousness of the person reading its pages. Unless otherwise indicated or inferred, when we use the term "soul," we are generalizing and referring to the entire immaterial essence of man.

The Webster's Dictionary defines soul as:

"The immaterial essence, animating principle, or actuating cause of an individual life," and also as the *"spiritual principle embodied in human beings, all rational and spiritual beings, or the universe."*

It also defines the soul as the *"person's total self."*

According to religion and philosophy, the soul is the immaterial part or essence of the microcosmic man that provides a sense of self and being—a sense of being an independent being, separate from the external environment.

In essence, religious philosophical philosophy believes that the soul is eternal. This doctrine is advocated by several schools of philosophy, including Neoplatonism.

St. Augustine, theologian and prelate, and Cicero, the Roman orator, both believed in the immortality of the soul. The soul is frequently confused with the mind or consciousness.

Theology expands on the foregoing definitions by understanding the soul to be divine in nature and capable of surviving the bodily form's disintegration.

Survivalism is the modern term for the belief in soul survival. Certain schools of metaphysics go on to say that the soul or spirit is a spark or emanation of the Source of all things, and that it is an evolving feature of the microcosm striving for apotheosis or deification.

Perhaps it is unnecessary to state that the soul-concept is subjective. It makes no difference whether it exists or not: no one has ever objectively observed the Self or soul as an essence.

What psychics or the typical individual perceive as phantoms or ethereal forms during particular psychological states are possibly the sheaths enshrouding the spiritual essence. What are we if we have a soul? What is "it" that is said to have a soul or Self? Is it possible for a Self to possess another Self? Is it possible to distinguish the soul from the Self? We cannot begin to fathom the immaterial man unless we recognize that he has multiple aspects.

In this regard, Occultism, Mysticism, Ancient Wisdom, and Metaphysics in general are far ahead of the information acquired by exoteric Religion, Philosophy, and Science.

The soul is not completely defined. We can generalize and say that the soul is man's immaterial aspect; yet this non-substantial feature of man is made up of different components, not all of which are immediately apprehensible by the various faculties of the intellect.

Furthermore, our information conveyance media, such as words, signs, and symbols, are incapable of relaying the entire truth as it is.

The divine aspect of immaterial man cannot be articulated in language or developed into ideas. A faculty of a lower aspect of the microcosm is incapable of fully comprehending a higher aspect. It is required to utilize the abilities linked with the microcosm in order to understand a higher aspect of it.

For example, the adage "it takes a thief to catch a thief" perfectly describes and supports our claim. Nobody knows a thief like another thief. Similarly, in order to understand anything, we must be that thing or function at its level. This metaphysical principle has a wide range of applications, and its implementation can result in a variety of occult experiences.

Although the academic definition of the soul is given above, there is no universal agreement or understanding of the terms "soul" and "spirit," as well as the other spiritual ideas taught in the various religions, sects, and cults. This lack of standardization produces misunderstanding, which frequently leads to pointless heated debates and even physical fights.

Some metaphysical systems see the preceding terminology as antiquated, and instead use specific words to denote the various parts of the soul or spirit.

Religion would be more aligned with God's purpose and attract more adherents if it updated its vocabulary and beliefs to reflect modern scientific findings and pure spiritual teachings of mysticism; as it stands, true religion appears to be wilting in God's temples. This assertion may be challenged, but those who do so may not comprehend what true religion is.

    The personality, conscience, emotional feelings, mental faculties, Ego, memory, various levels of consciousness, and volition are only a few of the many qualities of the soul. This is something that philosophy, theology, and metaphysics all agree on.

Religious and Ancient Beliefs of the Soul

Religious Beliefs

When we talk about religious beliefs, we're talking about theological tenets. Christianity and Islam share ideas and beliefs that have their origins in Judaism. Many of the concepts and beliefs of this religion were derived from the Persians, Egyptians, Babylonians, Chaldeans, and Sumerians. Perhaps it is true that practically every religion is syncretic, despite their best efforts to conceal this.

Eastern faiths, such as Buddhism and Taoism, are more mystical in nature and differ substantially from Semitic religions in many fundamental concepts; Hinduism, which includes numerous philosophical schools of thought, incorporates a wide range of theological notions.

Some Buddhist schools believe that there is no permanent thing known as the soul, and that what is perceived to be the soul is only a collection of karmic tendencies transmitted from one incarnation to the next. Their extreme ideas are nihilistic in character; nonetheless, it is questionable if this was conveyed in the Buddha's teachings. For example, if there is no Self, there is no Gautama Buddha; yet the faithful continue to direct their prayers to this exalted entity.

Although various religions have different ideas about the soul, they all lead to the One from which all sentient beings emerge.

Everyone has their own name or names for this Source, as well as their own views about this Divine Essence.

Theological precepts are sometimes polluted by the frailties of the human ego and intellect, and thus provide a weak foundation for studying authentic religion and its revelations about the soul. Nonetheless, we shall make every effort to present its principles with as little bias as possible. This section will be brief because doing the subject justice would require several pages and would exceed the scope of this work.

According to Christian theology, the soul prior to birth is devoid of any uniqueness or personality. Only when God breathes through man's nostrils does the soul gain self-consciousness and become a "living" being, and this state of being alive is thought to endure with the soul after death. It is written in the Book of Genesis:

"God made man out of the dust of the earth, breathed the breath of life into his nostrils, and made man a living soul." (Gen 2:7)

The expression "living soul" is associated with the state of being self-conscious. According to this belief, a person or being does not have a soul unless they are conscious of the existence of an ego, or self. A creature like this is "soulless." A human can be alive and full of the soul-essence, the life-force, yet nevertheless be soulless in the sense that it is not self-aware.

Some stages of insanity may depict "soulless" entities. While the living soul is related with ego awareness, immortality is associated with superego, or Higher Self, awareness. This, however, is the domain of metaphysical thought.

In essence, theology regards the soul as a thing placed in man. It is thought to be a divinely created being that is bestowed upon man as he takes his first breath. Christian theology developed the belief that man is a divine creation, the highest of all beings, and that the entire universe was made to support his existence alone.

The expressions "lost souls" or "degraded souls" are frequently used in Christianity. The moral quality of a person's life is thought to have an effect on the soul. However, from a metaphysical standpoint, soul-essence is perfect, immutable, and divine. Its conscious expression, rather than its substance, may be changed.

The consciousness derived from soul essence evolves and attempts to reflect the picture, archetype, or pattern created by God for man. This is stated explicitly in Genesis, but it is frequently read literally. This blueprint represents God's image or divine characteristics. It refers to the inner nature of the life-essence rather than its form.

In general, Hindus believe that the soul is an entity that resides in the physical body and is subject to reincarnation based on its karma. According to the Upanishads, *the Supreme Person, the size of a thumb, resides forever in the hearts of all human beings.* Its esoteric wisdom also tells us that the immaterial man is made up of numerous principles, each with their own specific function. The highest principle within man's microcosm is the Atma, also known as the Paratman by others.

Krishna, Arjuna, the carriage, and the horses depict the microcosm in the Bhagavad Gita. Krishna represents the Spirit, the highest aspect of man; Arjuna represents the expanding soul; the carriage represents the mind; and the horses represent the senses. Five horses are frequently depicted graphically. They represent man's senses, through which vital force escapes and goes wild.

The senses are repressed in yoga and esoteric practices so that the vital force can be directed within to awaken the dormant Arjuna. Krishna is the one who helps Arjuna with this project.

Ancient Beliefs

As previously stated, the belief in the persistence of the soul after death dates back to the dawn of humanity. Primitive Neanderthal tribes, for example, would bury food, tools, and weapons with their departed to provide them with the minimal essentials in the afterlife.

This habit is still practiced in some societies and demonstrates that not only is soul survival believed in, but also that the hereafter as a continuation of the type of life experienced in the physical world is assumed.

Prehistoric man's dominant belief was animism. Everything was thought to be alive and imbued with a soul-force that gave inanimate objects consciousness and intellect of some sort. Stars, in particular, were thought to be souls that had died and were now dwelling in heaven. The sky or firmaments were regarded to be heaven in the primordial imagination, much as hell was thought to be beneath the earth.

Because the soul "resided" and functioned in the corporeal body, a location for its home was sought. Some considered the heart to be the soul's organ, while others referred to the head. Some prehistoric societies believed that the blood was the soul's conveyance, carrying soul-substances to every region of the body.

In Goethe's (1749-1832) play, the demon Mephistopheles considers blood to be a "strange stuff." However, the concept that blood is the vehicle of the soul is not without merit. If the soul is taken to be the life-force, prana, chi, or even oxygen in this context, one can only speculate how the primitive mind intuited this scientific truth.

Blood transfusion has been scientifically proven to create a temporary change in character in the individual receiving the donor's blood. Is it possible that one's soul-characteristics are imbued in one's blood? Because blood was identified with the soul, many early cultures, including the Scythians, developed the practice of drinking their adversaries' or victims' blood in order to absorb their courage, strength, power, and talents.

The practice of making blood-brothers is also founded on a belief in the significance of blood as it relates to the soul and its transcendence above fleshly relationships. Members creating blood-brothers would drink each other's blood, forming a soul-bond that superseded conventional flesh-and-blood connections.

The ancients frequently represented the soul as a bird with human heads, maybe in reference to its ability to fly. Among the various ancient races, the Aztecs, ancient Greeks, and Egyptians, for example, frequently depicted the spirits of their dead in murals and pottery as a winged bird taking flight from its lifeless carcass. The soul was frequently represented by eagles, hawks, doves, peacocks, and phoenixes.

The seat of the soul was thought to be not just the head, heart, and blood, but also the breath. Believing that the breath is linked to the soul and life, the aborigines of Papua New Guinea would breathe via tubes into effigies of their progenitors in order to give their deceased souls some energy. This is a magical procedure that utilizes the law of resemblance.

As a last ditch effort to save their dying relatives' lives, many tribal groups practiced the placement of blockages in their nostrils. They think that doing so will effectively prevent the soul from fleeing and cause the body to die.

It is thought by ancient and primitive people that because the soul is related with the life force, illnesses or bodily weakness are caused by the soul's exodus from the gross form. In severe situations, the soul power was "taken" by an evil spirit, and it was the shaman's, the tribe witch- doctor's, responsibility to recapture the soul and restore it to the corporeal body. The shaman's capacity to separate his incorporeal side from his gross form is said to have assisted this type of work.

The Ancients' view of the soul evolved over time, and even now, our scientific understanding is always changing. Our varied ideas about the soul are linked to our various ideas about God. As man matures, so does his understanding of his soul and Source. Man has numerous views about the nature of his creator. In this context, it is clear that the phrase "God makes man, and man creates God" is true.

The Egyptians and Hindus were the most evolved ancient nations in their knowledge of the soul. We are specifically referring to their mystics, hierophants, and sages.

They saw man as a microcosm with multiple aspects, both material and incorporeal, each with its own role to play in the soul's life and destiny. Their numerous doctrines are still practiced in modern metaphysical-occult philosophy.

The great priests of the Orient taught many of the ancient Greek philosophers and sages such as Thales, Plato, and Pythagoras.

Scientific Views

Along the same lines, several schools of thought believe the self or ego is a by-product of a brain activity, but what gives rise to this function is unknown, and only an educated estimate is given.

The area of the brain that "causes" a sense of self has also yet to be uncovered. This concept of "brain produces awareness" is fundamentally the mechanists' worldview, which sees man as merely a machine. However, the above view is faulty because regions of the brain have been known to be damaged while still retaining a feeling of self.

For example, in the disease known as hydrocephalus, substantial parts of the cerebral cortex may be destroyed or missing, being replaced instead by cerebral-spinal fluid, and yet individuals suffering from such a condition may lead normal lives without being aware of their affliction. They may even have an above-average I.Q.

The mechanists, including Freud (1856-1939), believe that human behavioral acts are involuntary responses to external stimuli and that life is the product of the proper combination of chemicals generated from food and oxygen. They may admit that an animating force exists to vitalize the creature, but this force is viewed as a physical energy similar to electricity.

The mechanistic theory describes how perception occurs through the stimulation of the senses, which generates nerve impulses, and how these nerve impulses travel to the sections of the brain associated with the senses, where they form sensations; however, the theory does not take into account the true perceiver, who attempts to make sense of the sensations.

According to mechanists, the perceiver is one of the cerebral cortex's roles. In short, the mechanical view excludes the existence of the soul. A mechanist regards the alleged existence of the soul as a nonsense.

If the eminent neuropsychologist Karl Lashley (1890-1958), author of Brain Mechanisms and Intelligence, couldn't find the seat of memory in the brain after years of research, how much more difficult would it be to find the seat of the self or soul—despite Descartes' (1596-1650) assertion that the pineal gland is its locus? This French philosopher and mathematician also stated, "cogito, ergo sum," or "I think, therefore I am," meaning that the Self emerges as a result of thought or as a function of the intellect.

Mystics, on the other hand, have demonstrated to themselves the possibility of transcending thoughts while continuing in existence, as well as having an exalted sense of Self that is unified with the Cosmos.

Jean-Paul Sartre (1905-1980), a French philosopher and writer, agrees with the mystic. According to Sartre, existence is not dependent on mental activity, and a being does not exist merely because it thinks. Existence, according to Sartre, precedes the mind—or thinking.

Rene Descartes' remark is thus incorrect, or our interpretation of his statement is incorrect. "I believe, because I am" would be more accurate. Despite this, Descartes was partially correct in his belief that the pineal gland plays a vital role in man's occult physiology, as we will see later when we explore the metaphysical purview.

Mainstream science may deny the existence of the soul on the grounds that it is immaterial and so undetectable by their tools, but matter in its actual state is similarly immaterial. This was the claim of Leibniz (1646-1716), a

German philosopher who saw matter as a manifestation of Thinking—"a stupid kind of mind."

To illustrate this vividly, what we term concrete substance is actually made up of moving molecules. Molecules are made up of spinning atoms, which are made up of even smaller particles. If these subatomic particles were amplified, "nothing" would be discovered. Matter is thus composed of "emptiness." This emptiness may be referred to as "energy," "thought," or "spirit," but the reality remains that matter is as insubstantial as the soul. If one's reality is accepted, why not the other?

This "nothing," or emptiness, fills the numerous particles that make up matter. Another interesting point is that if we removed the space inherent in a human body, for example, and all the "particles" combined, the complete compaction would result in a piece of matter no larger than a mote of dust.

The ideas of Ralph Waldo Emerson (1803-1882), an American Transcendentalist, reflect Leibniz's thesis. Matter, according to Emerson, is "a phenomenon, not a substance." He also thought of the material world as:

"a divine dream, from which we may presently awake to the glories and certainties of day."

Nothing is destroyed, according to science. That matter is simply energy with a certain structure and magnetic field. It is widely known that everything in the universe is made entirely of energy. Because the existence of consciousness and a sense of self is indisputable, they should also be considered indestructible, as Science has previously hinted in its equations.

So, why does Science reject the possibility of disembodied consciousness—the soul? - because it is imperceptible? Really, it's an absurdity—even while embodied, the Self cannot be seen Can you see your Self?

Where does the concept of self-identity come from? Mainstream science appears to be a long way from figuring this one out. However, new paradigms are being developed by open-minded scientists who are combining the worldview of eastern mystics with contemporary breakthroughs and discoveries in physics and psychology.

Quantum physics and transpersonal psychology ideas are bridging the gap between essential religion and conventional science. Concerning the mystery of the Self in relation to the brain, we recall the words of researcher and scientist George Buletza, who stated in the Rosicrucian Digest (September 1983):

"Rather than the brain producing Self, it is the other way around. The brain is a product of Self, of Being ever striving to be. The brain is the incredibly fine instrument created by Self in the process of expressing its own nature . . ."

Many laboratory investigations throughout the world have revealed that human consciousness has the power to extend itself beyond the limitations of the brain and body, allowing it to perceive or affect events in faraway places. Some scientific observers believe that such mental activity implies that consciousness may exist independently of the bodily form.

Many fields of research, including physics, psychology, astrophysics, and biology, are investigating the soul, each with their unique techniques of investigation. Parapsychology is, in some ways, the most important branch of science that has emerged in recent years.

Parapsychology

The study of the nature of psychic or paranormal experiences is known as parapsychology. Its area of inquiry includes ESP, hauntings, poltergeist activity, near-death experiences, out-of-body experiences, UFOs, Strange Creatures, Weird Phenomena, and so on.

There are now numerous institutes dedicated to researching, studying, and teaching this field of knowledge. The term "parapsychologist" is frequently misused. Many people appear to believe that being a parapsychologist equates to being psychic. This is incorrect. A psychic may or may not be a parapsychologist.

A psychic is someone who perceives impressions through higher senses that the physical senses do not normally record. Psychics may not grasp the impressions they register and may trust and be deceived by illusions and appearances.

A parapsychologist aims to comprehend strange experiences by scientific analysis and empirical approaches utilizing carefully constructed instruments.

A mystically inclined metaphysician, on the other hand, tries to comprehend reality using his intellect, intuition, and other higher capacities. The basic procedures of the parapsychologist are three-dimensional, those of the psychic are four-dimensional, and those of the mystic-metaphysician are five-dimensional or higher.

We shall only show one example of many to demonstrate the distinction between a paranormal and a metaphysical interpretation of occurrences. As an example, if a psychic receives indications of an imminent tragedy, he will accept them as true and broadcast them to others. He'd make all sorts of forecasts based on the impressions that had formed in his mind. He would regard it as a divine revelation.

The metaphysician, on the other hand, perceives the perceptions received to be thought-forms-mind creations of terrified entities, having knowledge of Cosmic and natural laws. Man transmits thoughts, and psychics receive these thoughts, which may or may not be true. The unpleasant reality is that thoughts are creative.

What we think about with great feeling tends to manifest. So often, frightening forecasts come true; however, this does not have to be the case. We must learn to overcome fear. When psychics make predictions, they engender and amplify dread in the public. This is a vicious circle.

When psychics make people afraid, they begin to picture more catastrophic horrors, and these thoughts radiate out to vulnerable psychics, who repeat the process. The momentum gradually builds up to the point where it emerges physically.

However, let us not stray too far from our topic and return to it: Parapsychology has generated several research pathways for determining the reality of the soul and the survival of personal awareness. Although their findings are ambiguous by mainstream scientific standards, parapsychologists have been effective in obtaining data and essential knowledge that, when studied, appears to corroborate the age-old belief in the existence of the soul and its survival of bodily death.

Nonetheless, parapsychologists have developed a variety of theories to explain their findings, not all of which are consistent with the traditional notion of the soul.

It is also worth noting that the term "soul" is not commonly employed in mainstream science or parapsychology. Instead, the terms "mind," "consciousness," and "personality" are frequently used.

Metaphysical Viewpoints of the Soul

Near-Death Experience (NDE); Out-of-Body Experience (OBE); Bio-magnetic Radiation/Field (aura); Hauntings; Possessions; Bilocation; Past-Life Regression, and ESP are the numerous fields of parapsychological inquiry relating to the soul.

Many equipment and procedures are employed in the study of psychic phenomena. Hypnosis is frequently used to elicit subconscious information about a subject. A similar procedure has been used to successfully regress a person to a previous life and even between lifetimes. As a result, much knowledge about the afterlife and the soul's continuous existence has been gained.

Seances, the Ouija board, the planchette, automatic writing, and the pendulum are examples of unconventional ways that profess to contact disembodied intelligence; some of these methods are akin to the Indonesian Jailangkung and Nini Towok.

C.D. Broad (1887-1971), a former president of the Society of Psychical Research, felt that paranormal research would eventually reveal that psychological events may transcend physical death. He proposed that man possessed an invisible constituent, which he referred to as the psi-component, or "psychogenic factor." Parapsychology has made significant progress since the days of Broad.

Metaphysical Viewpoints

When discussing metaphysical ideas, questions about the origins of these teachings may arise. In general, metaphysical tenets are obtained from esoteric transmissions of lofty entities to select members of the human family. These beings have already progressed far beyond the human realm and its apex—the ideal human being as portrayed by the figure Adam Kadmon.

These lessons are founded on their personal experiences and comprehension of the Universal Truth. Some of these lofty beings' followers were able to verify, again via personal experience, a portion of the lessons transmitted by these Spiritual Masters. From the student's point of view, this would render portions of metaphysical teachings speculative or hypothetical.

There are also metaphysical doctrines that have been developed intellectually by pupils without first seeing its truth experientially, and hence may lack a foundation in reality. This is why certain metaphysical doctrines are constantly developing. Please keep this in mind.

A casual examination of metaphysical concepts reveals that they are as different as the many hypotheses created by science or theology; nonetheless, they all share a similar thread in that the soul, or spirit intellect, is seen as a distinct part of the human organism with a divine origin.

One of the most fundamental truths in contemporary metaphysics is that there is only

One Substance, One Power, One Life, One Mind, One Law in the entire Universe, and each being is a part of that One in its innermost "I AM" core. This is the foundation for all other metaphysical laws and truths. However, the preceding statement is not totally correct.

We referred to the One as existing in the Universe when, in fact, the opposite is true. The Universe is either a part of the One or a partial manifestation of the One.

Everything, according to the metaphysician, has a divine origin and is basically eternal. We stress the word "basically," since there is a distinction between form and expression and heavenly essence. For example, we can compare the essence to electricity, the form to an electric bulb, and the clarity and power (wattage) of the bulb to its representation.

Electricity, like the Spirit, the divine knowledge in man, is indestructible. The bulb, or human form, is fleeting in nature. The clarity and wattage, or power that it emits, is the growing component of man known as the soul.

The purity of the bulb, or the soul, determines the clarity. It is frequently contaminated by dust and filth, as well as negative emotions, thoughts, beliefs, and attitudes.

This image would imply that the Spirit is eternal, the form is transitory, and the soul is that component of the microcosm that strives to evolve spiritually until it is cognizant of its basic essence. It becomes everlasting by being awake, which means it is constantly aware of its essential nature. As a result, the soul is only potentially immortal.

Following our previous assertions, it should be realized that the soul-concept is constantly evolving, whether from a scientific, theological, philosophical, or metaphysical standpoint.

One could argue that truth is timeless, and that what was true in the past is also true in the present and future. We agree, but the issue here is man's concept of reality and how information is presented, not truth itself.

Metaphysics can be understood intellectually, which has limitations, or mystically, which delivers actual knowledge that the mind has difficulty evaluating, structuring into ideas, and putting into words.

According to one school of metaphysical thought, the soul is a function or development of the vital life energy that animates all living beings. This essential life force pervades the entire cosmos.

Matter is changing to the degree where it can sustain life, and living beings are evolving to the point where they can support the emergence of self-consciousness, which we refer to as "the soul." However, this does not imply that souls are dependent on matter to exist. They are linked to the universe's vital principle.

Some scientists consider the universe to be a living body or a living concept, rather than a dead or mechanical entity. The soul or self-consciousness can be viewed as a higher expression of the universal life-force.

This means that the soul is a dynamic potential that exists within energy. In the same way that energy is indestructible, the soul is in essence indestructible. As energy is kinetic, always in motion, so the soul's expression is never the same—it always evolves.

According to esoteric teachings, the microcosm is divided into three, five, or even seven aspects. Personality, Soul, and Spirit are the three divisions; or, in Indonesian, Jiwa, Roh, and Sukma—but remember, as we already stated, there is no conventional agreement on the names employed. Sukma can be named "Ingsun," "Atma," "the Self," or anything else. In this setting, principles are more significant than terms.

The triple microcosm is known as Nephesh, Neshamah/Ruah, and Yechidah in the Judaic Qaballa. In Buddhism, these are known as Nirmanakaya, Sambogakaya, and Dharmakaya. Personality, Ego, and Monad are all concepts in Theosophy. Rupa, Jiwa, and Atma are Hindu deities. In ancient Egypt, it was known as Khat, Ka, and Ba.

These three divisions are further subdivided. Certain Hindu scriptures divide them into five categories. According to Theosophical and Rosicrucian beliefs, the microcosm is divided into seven parts:

The Divine, Life, and Human Spirit can all be regarded the Soul in the Rosicrucian system. The Monad is known as the Spirit, while the other lesser components are known as the Personality. Each of these microcosmic components exists in its own plane or dimension and is made up of substances from that domain. Each serves a specific purpose in the operation of the microcosm. Every component vibrates at a different frequency.

Vibrations can be heard, seen, or felt as sound, light, or color. As a result, the seven components of the microcosm form a musical chord or a specific color—the amalgamation of all the colors of the components. This aggregate sound or hue is known as our "soul" name. Depending on one's soul growth, this sound might be dissonant or harmonious.

Each microcosm vibrates at a particular frequency; no two microcosms are exactly alike, just as no two snowflakes have the same pattern. Each microcosm component has a main faculty. The intellect is the Lower Mental's faculty, the Higher Mental's imagination, Buddhi's intuition, and Atma's inspiration.

We will not dig too deeply into the subject because this is not a thesis on the occult anatomy of man; sufficient to say that there are many more components in the microcosm than those mentioned above that are vibrating at a frequency undetected by our present technological tools. However, we will examine briefly in order to provide a general picture of man's hidden makeup.

In addition to the seven major components of man, the microcosm, there is a thread that binds them all. This is known as the sutratma. Forces and impulses from the microcosm's highest aspect pass to the lower aspects via this connecting bridge. Reaching out to our heavenly Source creates another bridge known

as the antahkarana. This antahkarana emerges
from the microcosm's lowest level and
eventually ties itself to the Monad.

The etheric body of man is made up of "force
lines." These are the mental equivalents of the
physical nervous system. A power-spot is
formed where they crisscross. Acupuncture
points, minor and major chakras, and tan-tiens
are examples of these. Certain external forces
form in the etheric body of man. Kundalini is
among them.

Kundalini is the cosmic fire, the force that
has the ability to purify and awaken the
microcosm's lowest energy structures. When it
awakens, it flows through specific etheric body
pathways. Kundalini awakening is related with
several major pathways.

The seed atoms are another important
feature of the microcosm. These atoms are
physical, emotional, and mental traces of the
soul's evolutionary history. They also serve as a
repository for our karmic tendencies,
expressions, and recordings.

Despite the fact that each of the seven
components of the microcosm has its own seed,
only three are usually considered in esoteric
texts. The Physical Seed-Atom, Emotional
Seed-Atom, and Mental Seed-Atom are the
three. Each of these seed atoms has a specific
location within the physical body. The pineal
gland contains the mental seed atom, which
appears to be where human awareness is
focused. As can be shown, Descartes was not
wholly incorrect in supposing that the pineal
gland was the seat of the soul.

As previously stated, the seeds are
recordings. They may be considered our
recording angels. They keep track of everything
we think, feel, and do. Our karma is also kept
in these seeds, and when the moment is right,
they release the repercussions of the karma
that we set in motion in the past.

The timing of this is governed by a higher
element of the microcosm, the Ego, and our
Solar Angel, as well as the guidance and decree
of the Lords of Karma—those entities who aid
humanity in balancing and harmonizing all
karmic activities.

The pineal gland also contains a number of
other spiritual components, making it the most
important gland in the endocrine system. The
pineal and pituitary glands are psychically
complementary, and when they work together,
the consequence is a more perfect human
expression. They are not only present to secrete
certain hormones, but they also play a crucial
function in occult physiology. We regret that
this book can only say so much.

A spark of the Ego, Soul, or Higher Self can
be found within the physical heart. This is
referred to as the "Supreme Person, the size of
a thumb" in the Upanishads. This spark has
three sides in nature: power/will, love/wisdom,
and intelligence/activity. They are represented
by three colors: blue, pink, and yellow.

Although religion agrees that the physical
body is the temple of the soul, many religious
people have transformed their temple into a
tomb, with its resident dead asleep in the
darkness of ignorance. When performed
mechanically, outward ceremonies, forms, and

rituals provide no meaningful spiritual benefit. They may satisfy the emotions, yet they dupe worshippers into believing in their piety. Outward forms are only manifestations of spiritual reality within.

Understanding and living these realities is how one advances in a true religious sense. For example, conventional religion may require us to pray once a day or five times a day, but authentic religion requires us to pray constantly, "25 hours a day, eight days a week." Prayer is a state of mind and consciousness. It is not in asking for something, but in understanding that everything we could possibly want is ours and is being done to us right now.

To summarize, Religion is Mysticism that is poorly understood, while Science is its child that is maturing. More could be said about this, but it would deviate from our main topic.

Origin of the Soul

The Monad is man's core being. The SELF is the God within Man. Its nature is Sat-Chit-Ananda, which translates as Existence, Consciousness, and Bliss. The Monad is a spark of the Divine Flame, the One Existence. The Monad is an emanation, not a creation. It is God personified within the microcosm.

The Ego, also known as the Soul, is an emanation of the Monad, while the Personality is an emanation of the Soul. The physical body is "created" by the Soul.

Everything is a manifestation of the One. IT takes the form of energy. Energy is everywhere, all-powerful, and all-knowing. It is unbreakable and eternal. Man is made up of energy, just like everything else. He possesses magnetic fields and structures that are all made of energy.

In a qualitative sense, the Monad within man is of God and is God. The Monad is only a minuscule fraction of the infinite whole.

When man recognizes his divine SELF-nature, he encounters the inner essence, the God within, and vows "unification" with his Source.

He knows that he is fundamentally "God"—but keep in mind that this refers to the God nature within rather than God's fullness, to the essence of man rather than his physical form or false ego. He says, like Jesus Christ, "I and my Father are one." This is not blasphemy, contrary to what theology may teach. It is the realization of our Source's love for us, who has given ITs very being upon us. IT has provided us with our identity.

This concept may be unfathomable to others, but it is a Truth shared by mystics of all generations and nations. God and Man, as well as God and the Universe, are inseparable. God is both immanent within and transcendent of all.

Man's fall from divine grace is the forgetfulness of this divine unity. Man ate the forbidden fruit of intellectual knowledge and lost touch with his true essence. As a result, his being was densified, and he was forced to wear "animal skins," i.e., the physical body.

Man's innermost existence is Light, but he descended into the lower dimensions due to ignorance. Each spatial decline encased his light in a bigger and thicker vestment until, in the three-dimensional universe, he wore animal skins and ensnared himself in matter—the most dumb part of the Mind, as Leibnitz put it.

The original sin of man is ignorance and forgetfulness. Let he who would hear hear!

The Soul's Purpose: Evolution

Change is a universal rule that results in the cycles of creation/destruction, involution/evolution, and so on. The Monad, a spark of the One, is divine in essence. It has a heavenly collective consciousness but has no awareness of individuality or separation from its Source. It was, however, created for a reason by its Progenitor.

It was manifested as a focus point of the One Being so that the One might experience diverse facets of Itself, growing in awareness of ITs inner potentiality, nature, and power. To accomplish so, it had to further densify ITs being to the lowest dimensional reality imaginable. This is an example of involution. As a result, the Monad emitted a triple Soul, which manifested the four lower bodies: physical, etheric, astral, and lower mental.

Man has completed the involutionary cycle and is now on the ascendant. Humanity is currently on an evolutionary road as part of its soul-journey and mission.

Human consciousness evolved through numerous lesser awareness levels, symbolized by the consciousness of minerals, plants, and animals, until it eventually acquired human-consciousness.

What is the final destination of the soul's journey? It most likely does not. Evolution in the school of life, as well as spiritual and cosmic growth, has no end. We may say that the goal is to unite with God, but that is just half of the story.

Words cannot convey what happens beyond that, and neither can the intellect. The universe does not have absolute inertia. Galaxies are born and galaxies die in an endless cycle.

By achieving God-Consciousness, or a higher consciousness level, one ascends to even higher spiritual heights that are beyond human comprehension.

The human kingdom is not the pinnacle of success; boundless possibilities await the expanding soul. All things are possible with God, and God is partly within our being, experiencing all things through us.

We acknowledge that what we have written above is difficult to understand and controversial; nonetheless, keep in mind that we do not impose our ideas on anyone. Because it is difficult for humans to explain abstract notions with words, a debate on this topic is unnecessary.

What we have discussed above are just the essential elements of the soul's purpose and cosmic journey, and should not be taken as the entire truth. It is only a portion of the truth. The study of cycles, rhythms, spiritual races, and so on would take us deep into the issue of the soul's purpose.

There are two aspects of evolution to consider: form evolution and awareness evolution, as well as two elements of the soul to consider: soul essence and soul manifestations. When we talk about evolution, we're talking about the consciousness component and the expression of the soul's inner divinity.

A complex neurological system and brain are required to sustain a higher expression of the Soul, or sense of Self, and an even larger unfoldment is required to sustain a higher type of consciousness known as "Christ Consciousness" or "Cosmic Consciousness." However, this is tied to organic development.

Darwinism's evolution pertains to the form component of life and does not need to be discussed further in this paper except to remark that what Darwinism refers to as evolution may just be an instance of adaption or genetic mutation.

We mentioned "soul-essence" and "soul-expression" earlier. The inner essence of the soul is God-essence. It possesses all of God's abilities, qualities, and potentialities.

All of God's traits are encoded into the soul's fundamental essence, just as the human blueprint is encoded in the DNA of every cell of the physical body.

Though the fundamental nature of the soul is divine, its expression or personality is ever-changing. While in physical form, the soul has the dual responsibility of cleaning up the stains on its personality and awakening its inner divine being so that its expression reflects the perfection of its essence.

Age of the Soul

Although spirit essence is ageless and immortal in general, souls can be classified based on their progressive unfoldment or development.

We do not discuss the origin of the soul here since, according to some occultists, not all human souls formed at the same "time" or from the same imaginary location in space.

This worldview holds that not all persons are of the same spiritual race. Our numerous racial conflicts stem from the depths of our hearts, where our metaphysical blueprints are diverse and heterogeneous.

Our sites of origin are identified with specific constellations in the starry sky, according to the channeled teachings of the New Age.

The so-called age of the soul can be determined in a variety of ways, and there are numerous categories. These methods for evaluating the evolutionary stage of the soul help us to better comprehend human behavioral patterns and mental/spiritual variations.

Some of the different classification systems for soul growth are known as "the Caste-System," "the Planetary Initiatory System," and "the Chronological-Aging System." Each system has its own way of determining soul advancement. We feel that addressing the problem of soul-age would increase psychology's knowledge of the human mind.

The Caste System

According to Hindus, Manu, the father of humanity, founded the caste system known as jati in Sanskrit thousands of years ago. There are four varna classes in this system.

The highest varna is Brahmin, which includes priests and academics. The warrior/ruler caste, known as Kshatriya, comes next in hierarchy. The merchants and farmers—the Vaisyas—come next. The Sudras, or laborers, are the lowest class.

The "Untouchables" exist outside of the class systems. These are the Dravidians, the original occupants of the country that the Aryans inhabited.

This caste system still exists today, but its rigidity has created a great deal of civil discontent; thankfully, various political and social reformers have brought about beneficial improvements and repealed many of the caste-harsh system's regulations.

According to proponents of the caste system, each soul is born into the caste based on its karma. It is because of one's karma that one is born into a lower caste. Only if it improved its karmic situation would it be born in a higher caste in a subsequent life.

Members of one caste were not permitted to marry members of another caste. The option to advance was not available in such a tight structure. The lower classes gradually became the slaves of the upper classes.

Although the physical appearance of the caste-system is repugnant to the evolved soul's exquisite, sensitive nature, its substance is true. Spiritually, everyone belongs to one of the caste system's classes. In other words, our soul operates at a caste level and eventually evolves through all castes.

We are currently functioning at a Sudra-consciousness level, a Kshatriya-consciousness level, and so on. There are also classes above the Brahmin level in terms of spirituality. These are the noble souls, the men and women who have attained perfection.

In a nutshell, the soul begins its evolutionary journey as an Untouchable; this is the soul-stage in which one merely tries to live. At this level, there is no idea of sin; one simply lives according to impulses.

The Untouchables are a primitive and illiterate people. Their minds and spirits have not yet been awakened.

As a Sudra, the soul has developed an egoic awareness and begins to labor for self-aggrandizement and self-centered goals.

As a Vaisya, the soul becomes exceedingly ambitious and materialistic, seeking money just for its own cause. The Vaisya is just concerned with himself. Vaisya wishes to possess all that exists.
In contrast, the Ksatriya has developed a sense of duty. He wants to help people, but his efforts are poisoned by his ego, which is now acting in a subtle way.

The Brahmin has begun to repent of the various vices and negative qualities that have stymied his spiritual advancement. He has almost no ego left in him. He has a mysterious personality. In his head and heart, he frequently believes that he has "seen it all" and "knew it all." This causes him to dislike the mundane world, and he usually becomes a renunciate. The Brahminic soul is more interested in spiritual things than in earthly pleasures.

From the preceding, we can imagine a hypothetical situation in which a Vaisya is born into a physical Kshatriya caste or becomes president of a country. As a result, the monarch develops despotic tendencies. Someone who abuses the trust that others invest in him. He takes advantage of his position in order to own and obtain the world's riches for selfish reasons.

The difference in soul development as it relates to class can be seen in an individual's perception of the concept of power.

Each class has its own unique interpretation of the term "power." Inquire about the power perception of someone with a Sudra soul development. He will demonstrate his "muscle-power." The Vaisya, on the other hand, will proclaim that money or even psychism is power. Position, status, or office are all sources of power for the Kshatriya... and probably his sword as well. Brahmins consider knowledge to be power. A Brahmin was the guy who claimed that the pen is mightier than the sword.

Without a doubt, the higher spiritual echelons would consider love to be the highest power.

The caste system has four, five, or perhaps six classes, but they are not clearly distinguished. There is some class overlap in some circumstances. A soul, for example, could be Sudra-Vaisya or Vaisya-Kshatriya. Or, for a far more precise classification, consider each class to have four sub-classes.

Sudra-Sudra, Vaisya-Sudra, Kshatriya-Sudra, and Brahmin-Sudra are a few examples. The following sub-classes are Sudra-Vaisya, Vaisya-Vaisya, Kshatriya-Vaisya, and so on. This would result in a total of 16 sub-classes, each with its own set of features.

We may also see how the caste-system pattern fits with the microcosm's four-fold personality: Sudra—physical body; Vaisya—astral or emotional body; Kshatriya—lower mental (material mind); Brahmin—higher mental (the abstract mind).

The Planetary Initiatory System

To understand the planetary initiations and their relationship to the stages of soul-unfoldment, we must first define initiation and the institution that supports it.

The "act of inducing, initiating, or instructing" is defined as initiation. It is frequently ritualistic in nature and can be found in a variety of social ceremonies.

Fraternal organizations frequently give their member-candidates an initiation to emphasize upon them the significance of the step they are about to take.

There are numerous sorts of initiations in a human being's existence, such as birth, adolescence, adulthood, motherhood, and so on-all of these are stages of growth that are marked by specific initiatory ceremonies in different cultures.

These ceremonies are commonly referred to as rites of passage. In that sense, initiation is a proclamation or reveal of what one has accomplished or reached.

Candidates seeking occult enlightenment are initiated in schools of esotericism. Mystic messages are frequently delivered to the neophyte during such initiatory procedures. To establish his worth, the candidate was frequently subjected to tests and trials.

In Ancient Egypt's initiation schools, for example, the candidate had to confront the rigors of the four elements. These tests would reveal whether the candidate has the requisite qualities, such as sincerity, courage, resolve, perseverance, and so on, to advance in the occult teachings and keep them from being misused.

When these hard examinations were finished, the individual would be transported to a specific chamber where he or she would be subjected to "death while alive."

The high priest performing the initiation would free the ka, or "soul," from the candidate's bodily form via mystic ways. In these initiations, the initiated person is given yogic instructions to practice.

Most initiatory systems divide occult advancement into three stages, each represented by an initiation. These three steps are known as the initiations of Osiris, Isis, and Serapis in ancient Egyptian initiatory systems.

Planetary initiations are very different from anything we've talked about so far. Man is evolving, and each step of his development is characterized by an initiation. These initiations are frequently carried out ritualistically by members of the Planetary Spiritual Hierarchy. This Spiritual Hierarchy is the planet's invisible governance.

According to Ancient Wisdom, the Spiritual Hierarchy was formed around 18 million years ago by an extraterrestrial creature from Venus named Sanat Kumara.

This exalted being is the planet's god or president-director. He was the one who sent numerous creatures to come on the world stage to teach humanity the Way of Truth, Love, and Wisdom. Our avatars, saints, and prophets are these beings. Many of these beings now hold prominent positions in Sanat Kumara's spiritual government.

The Spiritual Hierarchy's aim is to lead and support humanity's evolutionary struggle to higher levels, to the fifth kingdom—the kingdom of the gods—and beyond. Their mission is to liberate humanity from all self-imposed limits and erroneous beliefs that prohibit it from achieving godhood, divinity, and immortality. The Hierarchy teaches everyone how to break free from the cycle of reincarnation and eliminate karma.

As previously stated, the Spiritual Hierarchy's several initiations correspond to the various stages of humanity's progress. These initiation rites can be given formally or informally. They frequently occur in higher dimensions, above the astral realms.

Candidates for these initiations have them in the Out-of-Body state, and they are generally remembered during the waking state as a "lucid dream."

The mineral level is where life consciousness begins. It advances to the plant kingdom, then to the animal kingdom, and lastly to the human stage.

The human kingdom is divided into evolutionary stages. Most people have passed through the early primitive stage of humanity's collective evolution—and when we say "primitive," we mean in terms of consciousness rather than form.

As a result, the Hierarchy's consideration of mankind begins with the typical person. When the average person begins to spiritually awaken, he is referred to as an aspirant. This is comparable to the novice stage in any religious institution. The grade of discipleship follows this step.

A disciple is qualified for his first initiation after passing a series of examinations. This planet is related with 9 initiations. At each step and initiation, some soul qualities must be developed, certain traits and habits must be eradicated, and certain tasks must be completed.

The soul-development or expression of a person reveals where he or she stands on the evolutionary scale or spiritual path as determined by the Hierarchy. The vast majority of saints and prophets are third- and fourth-degree initiates. The fifth-degree initiation represents the level of the "Perfect Man".

In general, the first-degree initiate strives to resist and balance physical desires and inclinations. The second-degree initiate is concerned with purifying and balancing the emotional essence. The onus is on the third degree initiate to purify, develop, and transcend the mind. In the fourth initiation, the human ego would have to be removed or transcended. In the fifth initiation, perfection is accomplished.

What lies above that, the sixth-ninth degree, is beyond the comprehension of lower degree initiates and the general public. Between the two initiations, there are several minor ones, not all of which are ceremoniously celebrated.

The planetary initiations are represented by the numerous events in Jesus' life as described in the New Testament. This is a hidden truth that orthodox Christianity has yet to comprehend. The gospel stories are actually narratives of our own soul development and journey.

Not all initiations are completed in a single existence. As a result, a person may be born as a second- or third-degree initiate, a first or fourth degree initiate, or even an ordinary person who has not yet begun his spiritual journey.

Spiritually, our children may be more evolved than we are, just as candidates may be more developed than their seniors when they are initially admitted or initiated into a spiritual organization.

The Chronological Aging System

The Chronological Aging System is another approach for determining the age of the soul. This method gained significant attention once the text *'The Michael Handbook'* was published; nonetheless, this method is not new and has been taught by mystics throughout the years.

This approach basically follows the same chronological stages that an organism goes through during its life.

An organism's life begins as an infant and goes through the following stages: baby, youth (young), adult (mature), and elderly (old). The soul now passes through all of the aforementioned stages of development, and more. Souls who have crossed the "Old-soul" stage are regarded to be Transcendent and Infinite souls.

There are seven sub-stages or levels at each stage or age. The soul possesses identifying qualities and characteristics at every level and development, and these have both positive and negative elements.

In general, understanding someone's qualities can tell us their soul age and so where they are in their evolution. Below is a review of the soul stages and their essential qualities as detailed in the book *'The Michael Handbook'* published by Jose Stevens.

Infant souls are generally more concerned with survival than anything else, and they

frequently reside far away from the intricacies
of technological cultures.

Infant souls are thought to concentrate near
the equator since survival is easier and simpler
there. Infant spirits are violent, animalistic,
scared, superstitious, and illiterate. Their
redeeming characteristics include simplicity,
childlikeness, psychical abilities, and
instinctive behavior.

Baby souls are those beings who strictly
follow society's laws. They are steadfast in their
convictions and have a proclivity to succumb to
fanaticism, whether religious or otherwise.

Baby souls are at ease with formal rites and
ceremonies, and they strictly adhere to
theological dogmas. Baby souls' positive
characteristics include loyalty and obedience,
while their negative characteristics include
dogmatism, pettiness, and violence.

Young souls struggle to show their innate
individuality, their divinity; yet they do so
inadvertently by asserting their false ego,
abusing power, and manipulating others. As a
result of such approaches, they are frequently
the cause of conflict.

They are possessive by nature and are
preoccupied with concerns about power. They
want to be known and worshiped, and they are
frequently the success seekers.

Young souls are ambitious and competitive,
and they strive to be the best in their
profession. They are fantastic winners but
terrible losers. They are materialistic and
atheist in nature, and they are terrified of

death. They adore luxury and all of life's luxuries.

Productivity and industriousness are positive characteristics of young souls. They are competitive, self-righteous, manipulative, and vulnerable to exploitation.

Mature souls are less materialistic than their younger counterparts. Relationships, cultural and intellectual interests are more important to mature souls than lower personality activities.

This is the stage at which the soul begins to seek purpose in life. The soul begins to experience an emptiness in its heart because all of the ordinary things it sought in the early phases provided no enduring pleasure. Mentally, it becomes more open-minded, introspective, and begins to ponder the nature of Truth.

Mature souls are loving, observant, and open to others—these are their excellent characteristics. On the negative side, they might be overly connected, overly emotional, and neurotic.

The Old souls teach and guide the younger souls. They are the most competent among human souls to show others the Way since they have experienced life and its many facets. They usually do not just have academic awareness of Universal Truths but have personally experienced them through soul-perception.

Old souls relish their freedom and have a strong sense of interconnectedness. To the Old soul, everything is inseparable from itself, and everything is a facet of itself. They perceive and experience God in everything.

Old souls can be difficult to understand from the perspective of young souls. The Old souls appear to be devoid of strong ambition, motivation, and excitement for earthly existence. They appear distant, hesitant, and aloof.

Old souls like unconventional spiritual practices and alternate means of healing. They are esoterically inclined, continually seeking the deeper truths of religion rather than submitting to its formality; they are more spiritually aware than any other soul stage's soul groups.

Old souls are skilled at selecting and expressing any of their past-life personalities according on the events they confront in life. They may appear dominant one moment and meek, charming, and innocent the next.

Old souls understand that life is a performance and that they are only performers performing parts. The Old souls, with their spiritual vision and mystical insight, are simply heretical in the eyes of Baby and Young souls.

Younger souls have frequently tormented and executed older souls. The Young souls tend to attack what they fear and do not comprehend in the Old souls, resulting in unneeded karma.

The Old Soul is easygoing, eccentric, kind, gentle, loving, insightful, intuitive, and harmless, to name a few positive characteristics. Although some "species" of old souls can appear to be unpleasant for various karmic reasons, they have relatively few bad characteristics and ego left. Old souls can be lethargic, strange, and unmotivated at times.

Types of Souls

Essentially, Baby, Infant, and Young souls do not yet have coordinated personalities, and their souls are frequently governed by their personality's lowest instincts and urges.

Mature and Old souls have more control, and their personas are merged and functioning under the direction of the Soul, the Higher Self. The soul's consciousness level grows with each stage and level. It gets more spiritually conscious. Almost all prophets had Old souls. They taught the younger generations, which they misconstrued and turned into dogmas.

Old souls cannot be spiritually guided by young souls. Young souls just believe what they feel is true, whereas old souls know what they know. Young souls speculate, but old souls perceive. Infant souls are thought to receive their karmic lessons by suffering, whereas Baby souls learn through pain, Young souls through loss, Mature souls through misery, and Old souls through horror.

There is one fundamental that should be grasped, and that is the appropriateness of action and expression of souls regardless of stage. It is acceptable for a Baby soul to act like a baby but acting as an Adult soul is inappropriate and retrogressive. There is a relationship between the three systems outlined above.

The eyes have long been thought to be the portals to the soul. This is an esoteric fact. The age of the soul can be intuitively perceived through its eye-emanations, the way it gazes, the force and quality that its eyes emanate.

Younger souls have clear, energetic eyes, whilst elder souls have a deeper, worn-out, experienced look.

The eyes of transcendental souls, or those on the verge of perfection, the Old souls, emit power, warmth, love, compassion, and sincerity. They frequently have a distant expression, as if they are peering into the infinite. They have eyes that can look right through you.

The prevailing soul age of a country's population has an impact on its social life, social mores, beliefs, and the preservation of cultural and traditional values.

The soul-age of a country can be seen in how its internal and foreign diplomatic affairs are managed, as well as how its people react in times of crisis.

A materialistic nation is made up primarily of young souls, whereas a mystically oriented society is made up primarily of old people.

Types of Souls

There are no two Monads that are precisely alike, just as there are no two Souls that are exactly same. Each Monad, Soul, or creature is unique, a distinct aspect of the One Divinity, the One Reality. Nonetheless, in general, the psychological features of souls can be roughly classified.

There are numerous classification systems for humans based on body type and psychological character. Physically, bodies can be classified as ectomorph, endomorph, or mesomorph, and psychologically as introverted or extroverted, for example.

There are also different classification systems in metaphysics. The astrological method appears to be the most widely used.

It's no coincidence that the Chinese and Western astrological systems each have twelve signs symbolizing twelve different types of men. According to esoteric astrology, this figure is incorrect.

There are 144 primary sorts, according to esoteric traditions. Exoterically, because the qualities of each sign, both Western and Chinese, have been well-documented in literature, we will not go into detail about them here.

Planetary types are still relevant to astrology. This is named after our solar system's planets, as well as the sun and moon, albeit the latter two are not actually planets.

The following are the positive and negative features of these planetary types of men (except the Plutonian, about which nothing is known) as derived from The Michael Handbook:

The Moon or Lunar Type

Positive: Calm, methodical, passive, patient, tenacious, maternal, sympathetic, and receptive.

Negative: Moody, introspective, cold-hearted, incommunicative, willfull, stubborn, unforgiving, depressive, and destructive.

The Sun or Solar Type

Positive: Radiant, creative, elegant, dignified, refined, innocent, fun-loving, and childlike.

Negative: Airy, aloof, intolerant, naïve, indiscriminate, greedy, and juvenile.

The Mercurian Type

Positive: Intellectually active, perceptive, witty, clever, versatile, and clarity of expression.

Negative: Inconsistent, impulsive, explosive, nervous, sarcastic, argumentative, and cynical.

The Venusian Type

Positive: Harmonious, socially warm, loving, gentle, non-judgmental, loyal, easy-going, and friendly.

Negative: Lazy, dependent, indecisive, careless, sentimental, and sloppy.

The Martian Type

Positive: Vigorous, energetic, passionate, decisive, brutally honest, heroic nature, and forthright.

Negative: Impulsive, irritable, pugnacious, defensive, quarrelsome, brutal, rude, lacking forethought.

The Jupiterian Type

Positive: Grand, generous, benevolent, compassionate, kind, loyal, caring, affectionate, and philosophical.

Negative: Self-indulgent, extravagant, conceited, wasteful, and craving attention.

The Saturnian Type

Positive: Paternal, calm, secretive, just, moderate, and self-controlled.

Negative: Immutable, inflexible, overly intellectual, despondent, severe, aloof, and feelingless.

The Neptunian Type

Positive: Spiritual, quiet, idealistic, imaginative, sensitive, graceful, and artistically creative.

Negative: Impractical, unworldly, uncertain, and melancholy

The Uranian Type

Positive: Independent, original, strong-willed, loathing restriction, and humanitarian.

Negative: Eccentric, rebellious, and deviant.

****

Aside from the techniques of classification mentioned above, the 7-Ray kinds have gained prominence in recent years due to the teachings of early Theosophical leaders and Alice Bailey's books.

The study of the Seven Rays is a complicated subject, and the Spiritual Masters have yet to divulge anything about it. Nonetheless, what has already been given to humanity in the Alice Bailey teachings is substantial, and understanding them requires more than simple intelligence.

Before delving into the Seven Ray kinds, it is necessary to address several Ray-related issues. We will endeavor to provide this in a straightforward manner consistent with our current understanding of the issue. What exactly are these Rays?

Energy is emitted by every item, entity, being, and particle. The Sun in our solar system emits enormous amounts of cosmic energy to sustain the planets and all things on them.

The Spiritual Sun, also known as the Spirit of the Sun, emits a certain type of spiritual energy. This energy has three aspects and four qualities, similar to how the physical light spectrum contains three basic colors and four secondary hues. Each component and feature of this main spiritual energy has its own set of characteristics.

The Seven Rays refer to the seven
differentiations of the Sun's main energy.
These Seven Rays have a considerably greater
frequency than what our current scientific
instruments can detect.

Every component in man's microcosm is
primarily impregnated by one of the Seven
Rays. One of the Seven Rays may dominate the
physical body, while another may rule the
emotional or astral body.

When the four lower bodies of the
microcosm work in unison, their ruling Rays
are coordinated by a single Ray. When this
occurs, three ruling Rays must be considered in
the microcosm of man: the Ray ruling the
Monad (the Spirit), the Ray ruling the Soul,
and the Ray ruling the Personality.

Each microcosm, or individual human
being, may not have the same governing Rays.
For example, one person's personality may be
dominated by the second ray, while another by
the third or fourth, and so on.

A study of these Rays can help us
comprehend the Soul's makeup, potentials,
shortcomings and strengths, eccentricities, and
karmic fate. The nature of the power assumed
in order to fulfill one's role in the cosmic
scheme of things can be thought of as one's Ray
type/s.

The spiritual, psychological, and physical
traits, powers, and virtues of the Seven Rays.
Each Ray can be expressed completely or
poorly, and thus appears to have both good and
negative attributes. The Rays, on the other

hand, are completely neutral in nature. Some
of these characteristics include:

The Seven Ray types of men are represented
by the: King-First Ray, Sage-Second Ray,
Server-Third Ray, Artisan-Fourth Ray, Scholar-
Fifth Ray, Priest-Sixth Ray, Warrior-Seventh
Ray.

We regret that we are unable to elaborate on
the Rays' teachings and how the basic data
shown above adds up. This would be outside
the scope of this book. Those who want to go
farther should look into Alice Bailey's teachings
and modern interpreters.

Soul and Immortality

In a religious perspective, immortality is defined as the survival or continuation of self-identity, self-awareness, and all of the soul's natural features and attributes after the "Great Initiation," as death is frequently referred as.

Some consider immortality to be a potential state that can be obtained by good actions and moral living; others believe that immortality is an innate state of the soul. The German philosopher Immanuel Kant (1724-1804) described soul immortality as follows:

"The immortality of the soul means the infinitely prolonged existence of one and the same rational being."

According to the above statement, Kant believed that souls would perceive and rationally understand themselves to be the same as they were in the mortal state.

Among ancient cultures, the Egyptians were maybe the first to believe in immortality. They devised specific rituals for the dead that would guide those souls through the myriad events of the afterlife, such as the Judgement in the Hall of Osiris.

It was believed that their angel of death, the god Anubis, would aid the recently departed in crossing over to the Otherside, where it would be weighed on the scales against Maat, or Truth, in the Judgement Hall.

The famous 'Book of the Dead' was a guide for the Ba, the soul, etched in hieroglyphics on the tomb walls so that the soul would know what awaited it and what it had to perform.

One of the inscriptions discovered on the wall of a Fifth-Dynasty tomb shows that immortality was a major focus in Egyptian beliefs:

"They depart not as those who are dead, but they depart as those who are living."

One of the exoteric reasons that the Egyptians mummified their deceased was the idea that the soul survived the body and would eventually return. However, the true reason for mummification remains unknown.

Their practice of removing internal parts and storing them in special urns demonstrates that they did not truly anticipate their departed to return to the same body and be revived within. They would not have drained the internal organs if the body was to be reused.

Mummification is similar to the present method of cryogenics, in which newly deceased bodies are frozen. Men have long hoped that future technology would be able to resurrect the dead. The natural longing for immortality drives men to keep the dead body. Men have long thought that a future life, whether in this dimension or in another, is feasible.

Cicero once stated:

"There is in the minds of men, I know not how, a certain presage of a future existence; and this takes deepest root in the greatest geniuses and most exalted souls."

Why is the immortality of the soul so strongly held in most religions and philosophical thought?

Man was thought to be a dual entity in ancient times. He possessed a concrete and corporeal physical body, but the ancients also acknowledged that man had feelings and thoughts, which were tied to an intangible aspect that they referred to as spirit or soul.

Furthermore, many supernatural experiences, including as hauntings and psychic encounters, convinced man that the soul was actually immortal and could outlive the physical body.

Another aspect that gave credence to immortality according to the ancients was that the life-force accompanied the breath when man as a newly-born newborn made its first inhale, and that they both depart simultaneously at the time of death. The soul was thought to be released along with the last breath. The soul was indestructible, just as the breath. The living body breathes, whereas the dead body does not.

Many cultures used the same word to refer to both breath and soul, or the essence of life. The ancient Greeks, for example, used the term "pneuma" to refer to both the breath and the vital force that animates man. The word psyche was also used to describe the mind and soul.

Another view of immortality holds that the soul was never formed and has always been, even if its consciousness is not as developed as it is now. There is no end to what has no beginning. Whatever had an inception is thought to have a conclusion. Plato depicts Socrates arguing for the immortality of the soul in the Phaedo.

The belief in immortality is thought to be a direct extension of man's urge for self-preservation. All organisms battle to survive, to retain the life-force; all of man's finer instincts instill in him a sense of self-identity continuity despite the transitory process. It is human nature to believe in the continuance of life rather than its end. Man knows what the conscious mind merely has a hazy understanding of.

Spinoza stated in his book *'Ethics'*:

"We feel and know that we are eternal."

From a scientific standpoint, even if the soul survives the physical body, there is no guarantee that it will retain its integrity or structure indefinitely. For example, why do some theological doctrines think that the soul may suffer "the second death"? In what way? Also, when it is said that the soul is immortal, does this refer to its form or its essence?

If its essence is regarded immortal, scientists would agree, because matter and energy are interchangeable and basically indestructible. Nothing is ever destroyed; instead, it is converted or transmuted. However, the permanence of shape, structure—the structure of the soul—is debatable.

"Is self-identity and awareness related to the essence, function, or form of the soul?" is another critical scientific question.

Soul Faculties and Soul-Culture

From a scientific sense, the many theological speculations and theories concerning the survival of consciousness are without foundation.

Orthodox science is even skeptical of parapsychology's discoveries. Near-Death Experiences, spontaneous former life recall, hypnotic regressions, Out-of-Body Experiences, and psychic phenomena in general appear to hint to the immortality of the soul; yet, orthodox science considers such events inconclusive.

Fundamentally, science does not reject the existence or immortality of the soul; rather, it is now conducting empirical study to verify or disprove it. However, it is recognized that the phenomenon of the soul is difficult to objectively analyze.

Science recognizes the limitations of its tools in determining the existence of the soul.

Another part of immortality is concerned with the physical form. Physical immortality is a long-held belief that can be found in many civilizations.

The notion of bodily immortality appears constantly in mythology and stories. Most metaphysicians believe in the potential of its realization.

Many highly spiritually evolved yogis are reported to have attained the state of bodily immortality. We personally hold the hidden teachings that, according to our metaphysical preceptors, allow one to obtain immortality not only of the soul, but also of the physical body— at the very least, it significantly extends man's life-span.

Spiritual and bodily immortality are both carefully considered in Taoism. In terms of physical immortality, numerous alchemical compounds are said to immortalize the material body. Hsien are those who gain bodily immortality.

To the uninitiated, these alchemical formulations appear to be made of mineral or plant components; but, to the educated, they allude to internal chi or energy processes.

The spiritual realization of Tao, the Absolute, the "Mother," the "Source of all things," is related with the means for achieving spiritual immortality. Death, according to Lao Tzu, does not touch those who have discovered the Tao.

Immortality, according to certain spiritual beliefs, is the ongoing consciousness of Self-existence and being without ever falling into an unconscious state, regardless of psychological and bodily states or transformations such as sleep, concussions, or death.

It is the realization of one's divinity and oneness with the Source of all things. The divine Parent is related with immortality and the state of being eternal. One is not eternal until one realizes and is conscious of this unified state between one's individuality and the Divine Being; otherwise, one only

undergoes numerous changes and is subject to
the capricious forces of nature.

According to this viewpoint, immortality is
not something we instantly get as we pass
through transition. It is a state that we can
achieve right now. The realization of one's
unity with God is proof of one's eternal
existence.

There are various systems that claim to
teach the aspirant the means of gaining
mystical realization and oneness with the
divine being; they usually belong to the esoteric
sector of our world-religions; and, like religion
itself, some of these mystical schools believe
theirs is the finest. Many of the above notions
about immortality are prevalent in popular
philosophy.

The longing for immortality has also taken
hold of computer developers' thoughts.
According to these researchers, the computer is
equivalent to the human brain. They anticipate
that one day a supercomputer will be
developed in which every function of the brain
is reproduced, and that it will be possible to
transfer or download the human mind and
consciousness into it, so establishing an
artificial abode for the soul-intelligence.

This is their approach to immortalizing the
soul—"a ghost in the machine" reality. This is
related to the belief that computers and
microchips will become so smart and clever in
the near future that they will produce artificial
intelligence—that is, thoughts and feelings of
their own.

The soul possesses a plethora of psychic powers, the most of which are not employed by the normal person. The application of these abilities frequently results in unusual paranormal occurrences or phenomena.

The majority of psychic occurrences related with the dead are caused by the living. For example, many people assume that hauntings are caused by "dead people" appearing to the living, while in most situations, hauntings are produced by the astral forms of people who are sleeping and mistakenly appearing to others.

Clairvoyance, clairaudience, clairsentience, telepathy, psychokinesis, precognition, soul-travel, and bilocation are some of the psychic abilities. These psychic abilities can be enhanced. It is more than a present. Those who are born with them have frequently obtained them through psychic training programs in previous lifetimes.

The "powers" we stated earlier are thought to be the lesser capacities of the soul. These abilities are associated with the etheric, astral, and lower mental bodies. Higher spiritual faculties are related with higher components of the microcosm, such as Higher Mental, Buddhi, and Atma.

When left to its own devices, spiritual advancement moves at a sluggish speed. It may take millions of years for plant-like consciousness to progress to animal consciousness. Humans, in the normal process of evolution, would also require millennia to achieve human perfection or godhood—the next kingdom above humankind. However, there are spiritual activities that can significantly minimize this period.

What would normally take a million years might be completed in a single lifetime. The transformation of lead, which represents the imperfect human being, into gold, which represents the perfect man, was alchemy's most important secret discovery.

Why wait for nature to transform lead into gold when the process can be replicated and accelerated in the laboratory? This was the thinking of the alchemist. Exoterically, they were referring to metals as the topic of their change, but they were essentially referring to the human soul.

When the Master Jesus referenced the "strait and narrow path," he was referring to the acceleration of progress. Only a select few, he said, would discover this way. These are the teachings that the Master promised to offer to his pupils when they were completely ready.

These esoteric concepts and mystical activities have been "forgotten" in the Churches' current teachings.

There are many esoteric schools and organizations, both East and West, that are assisting mankind in rapidly evolving. Man is the only creature in the four kingdoms who has the ability to direct his own growth. Humanity would make significant progress if it collaborated with nature.

There would be no more wars or unnecessary conflicts if society as a whole reached the degree of consciousness acquired by the saints. This isn't an impossible task. Mortal, human thinking leads us to believe in our limitations, which do not exist.

Soul culture enables us to rapidly progress and achieve the goal set for us by our Progenitor. There are three essential techniques to consider in soul-culture: meditation, energy-work, and soul-refinement.

Meditation

Meditation is the most basic soul-culture discipline. Saints, prophets, sages, and mystics have practiced it throughout history. There are numerous meditation techniques created for specific objectives. The Hindu yogis, like the Buddhists and Taoists, have their own methods of meditation. The Western Tradition has its own types of meditation.

The primary goal of meditation is to align one's conscious mind with one's Higher Self, Soul, or inner divinity. We talk and the higher Intelligences listen in prayer; we speak and the higher Intelligences listen in meditation. As a result, meditation assists us in receiving spiritual and heavenly impulses from God and our highest nature. True meditation produces inspiration and self-empowerment.

In more advanced meditation practices, we are gradually brought to higher and higher dimensions or planes of consciousness where we will eventually connect or become aware of our Spirit—the Monad. Western writers refer to this state as "Cosmic Consciousness."

An old scripture teaches us a meditation technique:

"The Self, the inner spirit, ever dwelleth within the hearts of men. Patiently separate Him thou from the cover of the body in which He liveth, even as thou takest off the blades of a reed-plant. Him know thou as pure and immortal; know thou, He is pure and immortal." (Kathopanishad, II. 6.17)

Energy-Work

Before engaging in advanced meditation techniques, one's entire force-field and energy-structure must be cleansed, reinforced, refined, awakened, restructured, and empowered. This technique is known as energy-work.

The physical body, chakras, aura, etheric channels, etheric webs, electronic belt, and subconscious mind are all components of the microcosm that must be worked on in energy work. There are material and mental toxins that have collected in the vehicles of the Personality that must be cleared, as well as karmic stains. These bad energies generate a slew of issues, not only in higher spiritual growth techniques, but also in everyday life. Much of our so-called bad luck is caused by etheric garbage that has accumulated on our system.

Soul-Refinement

Soul-refinement is required for evolution. To raise one's vibrations and improve the quality of one's force-fields, one must also polish one's soul-nature, or character.

It is a person's low character that generates and draws negative energies; therefore it would be counterproductive to constantly undertake energy work when the time could be spent on more useful meditational techniques.

As a result, in addition to energy work, one must also concentrate on spiritualizing one's character—getting to the bottom of the problem, so to speak.

This part of mysticism is taught in almost all religions—a moral standard is established for us to follow. However, it might be tough to live up to the expectations that have been set for us. We may consciously know something is correct, yet we are compelled to think, feel, or act in the other direction. We are experiencing internal conflict.

Metaphysics provides specific strategies for resolving this conflict and reshaping the subconscious mind with constructive energy patterns.

Conclusion

It is unfortunate that this work could not be presented more perfectly, and that it leaves more to be desired. What we've written in this book is just the tip of the iceberg. There is considerably more to consider than what has been addressed in this book.

The Ancient Wisdom teachings are a repository of metaphysical information, and we recommend that anyone interested in mystical subjects read it.

Certain facets and knowledge about the entire immaterial component of man, as well as the destiny of the Soul, are far beyond the comprehension and reach of conventional science and psychics. Nonetheless, there is much more to be said about the Soul, not only from a metaphysical standpoint, but also from an anthropological, psychological, philosophical, and theological standpoint.

As a result, we urge the reader to conduct independent inquiry and gather the essential material to gain a better comprehension of the Soul—not only intellectually, but also experientially and mystically through spiritual growth.

In the beginning of this book, we spelled the term Soul with a small first capital letter; here, we end with an upper-case letter. The rationale should be evident after reading this book.

One last piece of advice: **Know Thyself!**